at least this i know

andrés n. ordorica

Contents

He that I love

Where I will burn

Epilogue

For you who has ever questioned if you belong,

these poems are for you.

November 16th, 2014

Come forward.

I pass through a corral,
my heart is in my throat.

Step closer, sir.

I feel the laser on my forehead,
I am ready for martyrdom.

Passport, please.

It comes out like hot bureaucratic vomit:

My name is Andrés Nicolás Ordorica,
I am reuniting with my husband;
Under Article 13 of The Freedom of Movement;
Under legal jurisdiction of The European Union.

Slow down, sir.

I am utilising Surinder Singh,
under the Immigration (European Economic Area)
Regulations 2013, Article 7 of the Citizens Directive;
Under legal jurisdiction of The European Union.

Sir, would you like to take a seat?

I will die for my country. Whomever will have me.
I will die for Ireland, England, Scotland, Turkey,
Japan, Germany, The United States, México,
The Aztecs, The Navajo, The Rarámuri,
The Celts, The Bloods, The Crips,
I will die for The Bears, Twinks, Goth Bottoms,
Those who are DTF, Unironic Aerosmith Fans,
Whomever will have me,
Spanish Conquistadors, Catholic Missionaries,
Nuns Back in The Habit, Vegans, Pescatarians,
Nut Milk Drinkers, whomever will have me,
Please, I belong!

Sir, would you like a glass of water?

I am ready for immediate patriation.
I am ready for belonging.
I am ready.

Please have a seat, sir, and someone will be with you
shortly.

Where I begin

Photograph

Summer light blinds my mother,
twenty-seven with golden ponytail,
curls set by that pink can of Aquanet.

In her cradled arms, me and my sister,
aged six and four, the three of us
sit still in an English garden.

Rose bushes adorn us as a tree
awakens its seasonal blossoms,
the sun feeding us its warmth.

Proper ladies sniff sprays of begonia
while observing our every move,
around us nature is neatly ordered.

We are three strangers in that place,
we wear shorts and windbreakers,
Nike high-top trainers.

We always stood out that way
with father and brother directing
from the other side of a lens.

A photo can tell so much.

Mother squinting, sister posing,
brother missing, father too.
Me burrowing deep into the earth.

Mother in the community pool

Mother rests on an inflatable donut,
her fair skin deepens in the afternoon sun,
she likes the water – *is a water baby*,
but is of the desert.

Mother ducks under the surface,
chemical golden, hair floating like tentacles
atop the glassy chlorinated plane,
until all of her is submerged.

Mother exists in all my stories,
her dreams that never came to be,
her words hidden inside me.

I write her into metaphor,
make her heroine,
mermaid,
immortal being.

Mother, she splashes me playfully
before drying off to have a rest,
lies recumbent on a plastic lounger,
curls splayed, soft and shiny, all around her.

[Mother.]

blessings

after George Mackay Brown's 'The Finished House'

the finished house
is holy water sprayed with olive branches
onto the walls and into the carpet

is my abuela taking cotton balls and silver coins
and tucking them into all the corners of every room
like some sort of mexican easter bunny

the finished house
is holding hands and speaking blessings
in a prayer circle led by my mother

the finished house
is toasting each other with mezcal and tecate
while carnitas bubble away on a wooden flame

but until you hang the crucifix
nailed to the wall – pride of place
the finished house is not finished

not until you say:
in jesus' name, amen.

For Papá
Para mi abuelo

It was July which in Chihuahua meant
you could fry a huevo on the sidewalk.

Copper-crimson, my skin was an artefact
of my Mother Land's history.

You wore your sombrero, cowboy boots,
the leather belt with silver repojado buckle.

You were an alondra belting out corridos
from a time gone by – a México that preceded me.

Between your honeyed notes, warm timbre,
I found our definition of love.

You showed me a different version of 'man',
offered me a choice between tender and strength.

Many called you 'oso' – a tall bear with leathery skin
and those beautiful green eyes.

But to me you were Papá.

The one who sang like Vincente Fernández,
but hugged liked the Holy Father.

Through the iron grille, on the other side of a window,
I watched you while my cousins played in the dirt.

You sang of victory and loss, of a love that stretched out
like a telephone cable across all our homelands.

In your words, I found myself and so I hummed along:

Love has no need for the cartographer,
because love has no borders,

Love is not a planet,
and so, it can never be destroyed,

Love has no expiration date,
and so, our love will always exist,

Love is a songbird that flies many thousands of miles
to find home in the heart of another.

Eventually, there was applause for you, for me.

As the sun set, the light hit the windowpane,
causing our two bodies to morph into one.

At once, I was a man in the reflection,
and you, you were a little boy singing.

At least this I know

They say the sun never set upon the British Empire,
I do not know if that is true.

But I hear it spread from ocean to ocean,
from green seas to waters blue.

They say that once a man flew around the world in
Eighty Days,
I do not know if that is true.

But I hear he did it in a hot air balloon,
wind guiding him from one country to the next.

They say Alexander conquered the world at quite a
young age,
I do not know if that is true.

But I hear all were under his rule,
from the Adriatic to Syria, Babylon to India.

I hear there is a place in a land far away
where chimney houses guard children from danger,
where fairies live near them and hide too,
I do not know if that is true.

They say that the New World is so varied and vast,
in one day, you can go from snow-capped hills to
great plains
where lakes are so wide, they spill into the horizon,
but again, I do not know if that is true.

They say there is a land with a beautiful rising sun,
creeping over a most holy mountain,
with hues of reds and oranges painting the sky,
a fiery phoenix ascending from ashen ground.

Who knows if any of this is true?

They say that while you are sleeping,
in a far-off land someone is waking,
that the sun sets in the West and rises in the East,
the moon pulls the ocean and causes waves to crash.

I do not know if this is true, but what I do know is...

My father once held my dreams in his hands,
while anointing me with chrism in God's name,
and although we don't share the same language,
in my father's eyes, I am loved.

At least this I know.

How I have grown

The sun is the only constant

The radiance of the sun:
its ambiance, its warmth,
the spectrum of colours
in a rainbow born of fog.

Pinks, lavender-blue,
greens, yellow-vermillion,
which only illuminate
when light refracts.

In solitude it stands,
unwavering, unending,
superior splendour,
a hanging arc.

The radiance of light:
its peacefulness and mirth,
a spectrum of colours,
the heat on my skin.

The sun is the only constant,
the rainbow is my friend.

Word association: Gay

Lonely	Longing	Searching
Anonymity	Isolated	Death
Painful	Abandoned	Deserted
Incomplete	Real	False
Kind	Top	Envious
Dangerous	Hidden	Angry
Hard	Masochistic	Raw
Excited	Confused	Capricious
Horny	Hopeful	Brave
Erstwhile	Soft	Bottom
Loathsome	Versatile	Scared
Lovely	Vulgar	Lust
Sinful	Optimistic	Deviant
Wanting	Wasteful	Weak

Breakdown on I-35

I am turning onto the interstate. I am attempting to check my rear-view and side mirrors like a safe driver. *Turn on indicator to merge into the next lane.* I believe I am dying. Not dying, but more so the idea of what it would be to die. *Check once more for any oncoming traffic.* Or more so what it would be to have something majorly catastrophic happen to offer my life a little perspective. I want something to live my life by or for or against. *Start merging into the next lane, please.* I am in my twenties and feel nothing great has happened. *Speed up a bit to keep up with the other cars, but not too fast.* I am too young to already feel like life has passed me by. *The merging lane will end soon so be quick.* Lately, I feel so tired. *Slow down a bit there are cops everywhere.* But then it feels as if I am on the precipice of my greatest work. *You can turn off the indicator now.* Only to be disappointed by my lack of success. *Remember the speed limit is 70...* I am like no one I know... *but if it is raining you should drop to 65.* I have tried writing my life's autobiography numerous times, firstly at the age of twelve and then at seventeen and twenty-eight. *Continue driving for another mile and a half.* I am neurotic. I am a mess. *Exit is the next right.* I am fleeting. I am unhinged. I am evasive. I am a coward. *Now continue down this road until you see the DMV.* I am afraid I won't accomplish anything great before thirty which is ridiculous, and yet. *Once you park, I will tell you your score.* I am afraid it will all be over too quickly. *Remember to put the car in park.* And, then what?

I am listening

I am listening to my heart more,
to the waves crashing in me,
to the orbital pull of the moon.

Yesterday, I took myself for a walk,
let the sun beat down on my skin,
looked into every crevice that I passed.

Afterwards, I took myself for a swim
dove deep inside my mind to where
anchors once weighed me down.

I swam past the delta's edge.
Something, or someone,
was pulling me toward its sound.

I began to swim further out
searching for that whale's call
which reverberated in the dark.

Yesterday, I let myself be still,
waded among dangerous silence,
finally acknowledged what I want.

Things I want

I want that freedom.
I want to be free, floating, and fierce.

I want to cut through like a machete, chopping down the
bamboo that surrounds me.

I want to walk into a room and be seen.
I want to see all things that represent me.
I want to see every shade and find solace in our
multitudes.

I want to soar high above and look down on this world
and find belonging.
I want to give comfort, receive comfort, comfortably exist
in the centre of it all.
I want to not have to think, not always question.

I want that freedom.

I want to swim far and wide.
I want to be a fish and swim safely in the sea.
I want to be caught in your net.

I want you to hoist me up, savour me: *your catch*.
I want to be gutted, filleted, and served on a platter for
your consumption.

I want to be free and wild and angry.
I want to be soft and hard and par-boiled.

I want you to eat me.
Now.

Bottled Blue

I want to capture Blue
bottle it up in its breezy
and effortless hue
take it with me on long journeys.

I want that colour to anoint me
wash me in Florida water
like chrism on my baptism day
cradled in my father's arms over the font.

That blue follows me
like a phantom balloon
whose helium never dies
long string tied to finger (a reminder).

Twenty-nine years around the sun
and that colour never gets old—
even if I do, bright as ever
and still moving.

It lives in the sky, the sea, mighty ocean
Blue can transport me back to happier times
can evoke feeling through memory
can transcend a lifetime.

When you look up at the sky
untainted by clouds or rain.

do you ever wonder:
why does blue mean sad?

For me
it means renewal
it means rebirth—
Blue is redemption.

Yes, I long to bottle Blue,
keep it safe forever
until the day that I need to share
with you some happiness.

Blue will be tied around my neck
wearing it like an amulet
I'll cross myself in its salvation:
Blue, the holiest of colours.

then and now

what did i want? to be the lead reindeer in the school
nativity
(but now, i would settle for happiness – read: healing).

i did not want to wear hand-me-down clothes, perhaps
thinking
world-renowned writers should not (i'm still unsure).

i wanted to not go to school, and instead to be on the
lakeshore
(and still now, i want to dive into that lake).

i was plagued by an insatiable desire to perfect the
origami crane
(now, i simply want to be warm).

it was my mission to get rid of long division – uninvent
it – but now?
i want to be on a balcony in barrio roma drinking beer,
dividing the time between dreaming and remembering.

i wanted to swing as high as a one-story building, now
to scream,
i wanted to learn to swim, now to drive for miles alone,
embarrassingly, or post-traumatically, to not get
spanked.

i still want this every now and then hoping it might heal
the past,
but now my greatest want is to be able to *kiss* my
grandparents

(so as not forget my past).

i used to want to be braver – part of me still does –
but if not,
if it is an impossible ask, then really, just to hug my mom.

i wanted to not play baseball, for my dad to be okay
with this,
but now what i want the most is to *heal* my grandparents.

as a young boy, i wanted to eat pepperoni pizza every day,
but now i would settle for dancing at a festival (as if i
were still a young boy).

i wanted to be good at sonic the hedgehog, now, to cry
for a long time.

back then, what did i want? *well to be an only child.*
and now, what do i want? *well to have a child.*

Birdsong

In soft early hours,
under Mother Nature's
omniscient conducting,
birdsong begins,
grass starts to rustle,
a breezy overture:

...and I am no longer lonely.

What I have lost

Things I think but never do

If I wrote you, like *actually* wrote,
I might write you in invisible ink.

Fill the letter with inside jokes,
if only to hear you laugh, hear you cackle.

I might include photos of orange marigolds
pastel pink peonies, billowy baby's breath,
all carefully arranged before the altar.

Script ancient prayers for you,
anointing them in the Holy Mother's name.

I would cry into the folds of paper,
then place gently in an envelope.

Spritz the letter in vanilla musk,
the kind you buy in plastic vials,
three dollars of gas station perfume.

By the seashore

When I ran into my friend, they shared the news.
Each word pummeled me, ripped skin, broke bones
– crash.
They repeated that curt phrase over and over: *She's dead*.

Dead?

I remember thinking *She's not dead* – but simply was not
returning because:

-She landed an amazing summer internship,
-She was going to travel the world,
-Because she had better things to do.

I did not understand that *She* wasn't returning because:

-Her car skidded off the road,
-Her car veered into the wrong lane,
-Because life, like a car, could be totaled (gone forever).

Many lifetimes ago, it was day one of high school and she
my first friend.

She walked right up to me,
tapped me on the shoulder and said:
Hey, come sit with us.

The next four years were of her making—
the highs and the lows: university applications,
rejections, betrayal, and redemption.

For four years, we were immortal,
we were laughing and dancing electric,
we were indestructible and the world ours.

When my friend shared the news,
we were standing by the sea.

I did not hear the words over the waves;
the sea was so beautiful and big and ceaseless,
and I not ready to say goodbye.

As the waves continued to crash,
I prayed they might wash over me,
swallowing me up in that moment.

When my friend shared the news,
we were standing by the sea.

Si Dios Quiere

Abuela sits on the other side of a telephone line
sipping café from a Mickey Mouse mug.

"I'll see you in a month, Mamá."

"Si Dios quiere, mijo. Si Dios quiere."

If God wants, They would want me to be
obedient, chaste, and ever faithful,
to remember to say evening prayers,
and not eat meat on Lenten Fridays.

But if God wants something particular of me,
I think They would want me to be
a rebozo threaded by an ancient needle
stretched out above memories that chase me.

If God dreams, They would dream me
as Abuela pins clothes to a line
under the midmorning sun as heat rises
off freshly scrubbed terracotta tiles.

If God imagines, They would imagine me
safely walking hand in hand,
languidly under summer clouds
as he whispers in my ear, *Te amo.*

If God transforms, They would transform me
into a brilliant butterfly, dancing freely over
fresh flowers, roses, hyacinths, marigolds;
sipping nectar in a drunken spring daze.

If God creates, They would create me
a map stretched out over mountains and seas,
water blurring the hard ink lines of borders
to carry me to places not yet travelled.

"¿Estás ahí mijo?"

"Sí, Mamá. I'm here."

If God wants, They would want me
to exist forever so Abuela always has someone
on the other side of an unbreakable line,
waiting to greet her like a son that never sets.

These pyramids are houses for the dead

These pyramids are houses for the dead.
Looking upwards, I find a point to pray to above the
pyramid.

Early on, I learned that death's an opportunity.

A calavera is a mask made of sugar and water
with colourful details but is simply a skeleton.

A calavera is our way of bringing back the dead,
the ones who live in pyramids.

A church is a pyramid of prayer,
looking up to the cross, I find a point to direct them.

En el nombre del Padre y del Hijo y del Espíritu Santo.
En el nombre del Padre y del Hijo y del Espíritu Santo.
En el nombre del Padre y del Hijo y del Espíritu Santo.

It's said this place is where my ancestors saw an eagle
with serpent in mouth.

My ancestors were told to find an eagle with serpent in
mouth.

In this place, you'll build an empire.
In this place, they built an empire.
This place was once an empire.

We once climbed Bennachie, your mother, you, and me.
We once climbed up it and saw the world below.

You had to pee you said,
but the wind was blowing hard,
we made you walk all the way around,
so as not to catch us in your spray.

Although not particularly high,
compared to other Scottish peaks,
it is very prominent,
owing to its isolation and relative flatness
in the surrounding terrain,
it dominates the skyline.

Maybe Bennachie is your Tenochtitlán,
but we just don't know it yet?

Maybe your ancestors built up the dirt
from surrounding terrain, and over time
rolled in granite stones, until one day
a mound was formed and then
a hill-cum-mountain.

Bennachie is very prominent,
owing to its isolation and relative flatness
in the surrounding terrain...

Like Tenochtitlán,
Like the pyramids,
Like a church.

...it dominates the skyline.

En el nombre del Padre y del Hijo y del Espíritu Santo.
En el nombre del Padre y del Hijo y del Espíritu Santo.
En el nombre del Padre y del Hijo y del Espíritu Santo.

These pyramids are houses for the dead.

Looking upwards from the terrain,
isolated and relatively flat,
I see a point to pray to,
somewhere to point my prayers.

My ancestors walked through deserts
and waded through marshland
before Tenochtitlán.

Maybe Bennachie is yours?
Maybe Bennachie is yours?
Maybe Bennachie is yours?

Untitled [May 14th, 2010]

So, it seems I have survived today.
In fact, the church bells are sounding
marking its end.

A year has passed since you left me
and I do believe I've changed.

If you could only see me now—
I wonder what you'd say.

> The sun is beaming down on me
> the heat permeates my skin.

> An ant, it crawls on top of me
> tunnelling within.

Rosemary

I came upon a sprig of rosemary
hanging in a row of five
tied with twine to a fence,
a sign that read, *Help Yourself*,
the smell of it ceremonial
reminding me of life's seasons

...and I was grateful to be alive.

What I have given

Amor

I am going to nurture him like a nopal,
make him grow pretty flowers
but remove his spiny needles.

Until he stands tall.
Until he is fully formed.
Until I can hold him close.

Then I will gather him,
take his flower and his fruit
and burn it all until
our love is something new.

Transform it into tequila, mezcal,
until our love is sotol, pulque thick,
raicilla crystal clear.

Like the drink, our love will be pure,
will burn our tongues and throats,
will bring the blues in the morning.

El vaquero

He was taller than me,
Miller Lite on his breath.

The bar thick with heat,
amber smoke hung in frame,
the floor lined by peanut shells.

His Wranglers were so tight
that I could see his muscles
contracting as we danced.

Men and women watched
with angry bloodshot eyes
full of stinging condemnation.

But I felt safe in his arms,
held firm against his longing,
aware of the power I possessed.

Faggot

Pinkish face – malt stained.
He had two kids (boy and girl).

They seemed used to this,
although still so young.

The croaking voice called, "Faggot."
Rang loudly within others' silences.

Berated us for existing,
each letter wafting in the air.

Until finally stillness pushed us
out onto the cold waterfront.

An evening stolen from us
by the man at the back of the bus.

Four men

I. Kensal Green

Sex swelling in the air as vodka surged through my veins,
I met him under sweet plumes of purple hashish,
appearing from nowhere like Alice's Caterpillar oracle,
he spoke in riddles which confused my better judgement,
we walked together into a quiet park, but the further we went,
the softer the Mad Hatter's party became,
on command, I got down on all fours like the dog I was,
barked and growled with each thrust, yes, I was a good boy.

II. Borough

It was a cool October Monday when I read his message,
I wandered for two miles from the station to his estate,
the room was in complete disarray when I arrived,
he kept the small chat small, the introductions none,
his finger pointed to a bed and I followed its direction,
the girth of him was painful, he never asked how I felt,
I told myself, it won't always be like this, won't always hurt,
sometimes they might even love you in return.

III. Ladbroke Grove

He welcomed me by offering a mix of loose-leaf tea,
poured steaming water from a blue China pot,
I read my fortune in the bottom of the cup,
he read the loneliness in my youthful face,
did not make me take him in my mouth as I had promised,

instead, he let me browse his many shelves of books,
and shelter a bit longer from the autumn rain,
we talked all afternoon amidst the droplets' patter.

IV. Unknown

My girlfriends handed me over like four fathers of the bride
to a handsome groom I met drunk on a Soho dancefloor,
he had a bald head, an Italian accent (or maybe Polish),
he drove us away in his Mini Cooper down busy streets,
all night I went in and out of consciousness from the liquor,
he and I were too intoxicated to promise each other forever,
when I finally awoke in my marriage bed, a blushing bride,
I realised I did not know my new husband's name.

Losing myself

I waited next to the neon lights
written in brush stroked Kanji.

Tap, tap, on the windowpane
clouded in humid condensation.

But, still your smile
shone through the opaque glass.

I opened my door, closed my door,
followed you across the street.

Takero like *te queiro*: I love you,
it's how you introduced yourself.

You told me to undress,
I did not fight your commands.

You proceeded to wash my body,
scrubbed soap between my legs.

Studied the shape of my round bottom,
told me what you planned to do to it.

Your tongue explored me,
and I longed to know its taste.

You filled my body with all of you,
taught me how two bodies move as one.

I wondered if it were possible
to break a body in this way.

When I left your place,
I could not be certain I was the same.

I opened my door, closed my door,
rolled down the window to defog the car.

I looked up at the neon sign,
and drew in the air, let it fill my body.

Exhaling as both the old me,
and the one about to drive away.

Newark Liberty International Airport

In a departure lounge
in the state of New Jersey,
the least beautiful one,
that's where I first saw you.

You were older than me
with beautiful blue eyes
lined with circles
like a trunk of sequoia.

Your name Adam,
meaning to be red,
meaning to make,
made from dirt.

Like the first man:
Adam my first man,
Adam my man-made
fantasy.

While the plane taxied
you asked me questions
of my travels to come
while I made up our story.

Blurring our present and future
with memories of your hands
tracing our timeline together,
tracing the outline of our love.

I dreamt of our first *good morning*
as the sun rose above the Pacific,
as the sun shone brightly on your face,
as I imagined you kissing me.

We'd talk between the midnight hours
over a meal which I could not say
was breakfast or dinner,
but would be our first together.

At the baggage carousel,
I would bump into you
tired but still enamoured,
happy to see your familiar face.

I would want to be braver,
want to invite you to my room,
want to feel your hands
span the time zones of my body.

But I'd simply say goodbye
as you kissed me on the cheek
and wished me well,
waving me off into the ether.

You see, I once met an Adam
seated next to me on a plane,
introduced myself to him,
did nothing to become his Eve.

The party

You – too catholic, too nervous for anything stronger than gin – bounce to the music playing off a laptop. In the guest bedroom, your friends cut cocaine on glass compacts, and smoke weed while dangling out first story windows.

1. He dances across from you.
2. There is a white Ikea coffee table between you.
3. A floor lamp with draped bandana casts pink light onto Him.

You look sun-kissed, exotic standing between shadow and half-light. Minutes pass before either of you utter a word, letting 'Super Bass' fill the space as you duke it out in a lip-sync battle royale.

He extends his left leg to the ceiling, you arch your back like London Bridge, He death drops like someone has removed his spinal column. You are fighting for your life, so you cartwheel from your side of the room to His. *Boom!*

The gin moves through your veins quickly. This is the most alive you have been.

He slowly moves toward you; you relinquish. He presses His sharp hip bones into your softer lower back. The hardness of His penis digs into you.

1. Your friends are taking too long in the other room.
2. The coffee table is no longer a buffer.
3. You now are both different hues of red, swaying in a corner.

You let His mouth blow warm air on your neck, you let His fingers run the elastic of your underwear, let Him take fistfuls of your pubic hair in His hands, but you instruct yourself on the one thing you still have control over: *You will not fuck Him tonight.*

Yes, you will not give yourself to Him just yet.

8 synonyms for vermillion

1. Vermillion is the strong clavicle of that man at the gym – whose grey eyes watch me while in front of the mirror: *convex, flipped inside his dirty mind.* His taut chest and razor clam collarbone peeking out of his dirty vest. He stands there imagining what it would be to spot me as I squat deeper into the pain of the weight I shoulder, imagining what it would be to go deeper to its source.

2. Vermillion is a sweaty drag bar at the corner of *Zarzamora* and *Congress,* where I wait to be picked up by a stranger; plucked like the desert Flower that I am, thirsty but elegant, ready to be sniffed and then discarded along the highway.

3. It is the colour of sashimi and flavour profile of umami – *salt of lip* – dunked in sodium: raw.

4. It is red-orange speedos that fit tightly around brown-copper quads and muscular bums with turquoise wet dripping off shaven legs. *Ready to dive deep inside.*

5. It is men from Seville who fuck apathetically, vigorously, languidly and who take breaks to smoke fags... *they call it a siesta...* while texting people not currently present in our bed as I watch on naked.

6. Vermillion; a metallic heat like a conductor of electricity – the pigment of childhood – my favourite crayon in the box.

7. It is candles burning in the aisles of TK Maxx – wasting time and smelling indiscriminately, searching for a bargain. *I am the Goldilocks of scent and colour.*

8. It is fire – or perhaps it is desire – which is not a type of flame you can simply strike with a match; it slowly burns until it destroys everything in its way.

fresas

after Edwin Morgan

fresas not diced
not quartered
simply destemmed
washed first
patted dry
primavera en la boca
mayo en la lengua
aftertaste of joy
no need to wash the plates
in the middle of a storm.

He that I love

Mountaintop

Sometimes over snowy mountaintops,
I think of the crevices in your brain,
question where your neurons meet,
wondering if synapses send signals
when you accidentally brush my thigh?

Longing to ski down the slopes of your thoughts
but fearing an avalanche of questions to come,
as you pry through snow to uncover my intent,
I hesitate, but the truth is you are a mountaintop,
and I, a mountaineer with a deep desire to soar.

Then I remember how humans were never
meant to see above mountaintops, and yet,
a deep desire to ascend is the human condition,
and so, humans were always meant to fly,
and I, always meant to see inside your mind.

The unspeakable type

I gave you what I never had: ███████
when you taught me all will be fine.

I counted to five then ten then twenty;
steeped the molten iron in cold water.

I learned to cool off from that red heat,
for fear my inner flame might cause pain.

You taught me how to manipulate the ember for good,
showed me how to bend the iron to make it soft.

In return, I gave you ██████ when life gave us distance.
I gave you ██████ when your fate felt uncertain, unclear.

You gave me ██████ when I was lost out in that storm.
You gave me ██████ when I needed to let go of them.

I gave you what I never had given to others,
but you taught me how to bestow that on you.

I gave you what I longed to give somebody.
I gave you all the ██████ I had inside of me.

and you promised all will be fine,
and you said that ██████ was enough.

Hove

We are on a train. You and I. Heading one direction, you facing backwards, I facing our destination head on.

These have become our roles. You comfortable in the unknown, me needing to be in the know.

You trusting of the universe's will, me needing to prepare for the unpreparable. For what probably won't happen. But, if it did, I have a plan.

It is only a train ride but to someone who knows us, it says everything.

So, as you sit bathed in blue light, I sit watching – I often am watching you.

You used to tell me my gaze intimidated you. This was early on in our relationship which was many lifetimes ago.

As I take you in, you tell of political news that is of great interest and importance.

You have always been this way – someone with a distinct understanding of right and wrong.

You list off names of MPs and secretaries, people who for a moment of my life exist.

These names and laws and opinions will sit at the back of my mind.

I will go about my life as normal, but now and again, they will come up. When watching the news or reading a broadsheet, I will remember how you first shared their names with me.

Will think of you and the white face painted blue. You explaining the change you wanted me to be part of, how you believed that I could create waves.

In my mind, you will be remembered as the master, my call to action, my revolution – I the pupil.

Out the window green is melding into other colours of the landscape as we zip down to the seaside. Announcements are made over the intercom. Such interesting named towns and cities.

Hove? a word that perplexes me. Origins of nautical yesteryears.

Heave, ho, heave, hove?

Bringing to mind images of muscular seafarers battling storms, crushing waves, pulling ropes and manoeuvring sails, all the while praying that Neptune will be forgiving.

You leave me at the beach, as you go into a dusty archive below ground.

So, I write you into stories that fill my notebook – weaving future truths for us.

In this story, I am a stranger in that place, left alone and so I wait for you.

I wait – thinking words and dreaming you in metaphor, making you a hero.

As I fill pages with new words, recalling how I heard "Hove" for the first time.

Heave, ho, heave, hove.

Yes, I remember it now. I am the boat and you my seafarer steering us evermore off into the distance. Over unchartered waters, where we will write a new story together.

When you are frail and can't remember, I will tell you it – that day I waited for you on a stony beach and wrote you into metaphor.

Neroli Kiss

They say iron girders dyed the river orange,
the one we sailed down that Indian summer.

My hand scooped up clementine
water only to find it was me

who was coloured that apricot pink
but still I supped the mystic drink.

While sailing down the river
my mind went with the currents

and I turned to you, full of wonder,
sun-stroked, open-mouthed to ask:

Do you ever stop to think how water
might have linked our dual bodies?

Coral springs, venetian seas, salmon riverbeds;
The Ganges, Rio Grande, the Don or Dee?

[or somewhere in between]

My mind poured out like a broken dam,
overflowing onto our afternoon:

Do you ever dream about a life
in which we never met?

Or wonder what would be
had I not traversed the sea?

[I hope you never ask these questions]

But, you smiled and continued rowing
toward something I did not know.

I looked to the city's riverbank
watching couples promenade arm in arm
and thought of that day.

Your lilted tongue, each turn of phrase,
capturing my attention along the Thames.

On the Clyde, I cupped my hands
in Holy consecration, offering you a drink.

You turned to me,
mischievous and said:

They say iron girders once dyed the river orange.

But I understood it to be myth,
still when I kissed your lips

a rusty neroli aftertaste
lingered on my tongue.

And in your eyes, I realised
it was the sun that was our constant.

The very thing we both orbited
all those years until our final first kiss.

There was a copper memory I left behind
as we continued sailing down the Clyde.

Perhaps, I'll return to it in the future
and find the blood orange taste awaiting me.

From the banks, I might see two lovers
sailing down the tangerine stream

And when I do, I'll wash in its
blessed blossom loch and think of you.

We are young and still have time

1. Heat on skin as the sun bores down
    on wood varnished by sticky sweet cider.

    Air smelling of spring, summer in the distance,
    I smile at you while soaking up the promise of a day.

2. We walk side by side along the gallery wall
    with its monochrome photos of distant cities.

    We say how we will go *there* someday,
    and we believe it because we are young.

3. Coorying in among the dim candlelight,
    pressed up against the foggy glass alcove.

    Seasons changing, the patio a distant memory,
    we laugh about this as we toast the year.

4. Friday night, I wait for you on the steps,
    ten minutes to go until the band starts up.

    We've missed the preshow pint (*no bother*),
    really, I just want your company in the dark.

5. Music blares from speakers stacked like Lego,
    as strobe lights cast blue-violet filters on our skin.

    The throng of revellers fall and rise against the stage,
    the band they are like ministers preaching to the
    masses.

6. Over the bass and drum, I whisper, *I love you*
   and through the snare, you mouth, *I'm glad
   we're here.*

   All around us, the future feels bright and
   never-ending.

   We believe it because we are young and still
   have time.

It had been so long

Opening the door
of a photo album,
I decide amidst quiet
to remember:

Remember what?

To remember
our wedding day,
how we flung
open the door,
greeted by music.

Walking side by side,
as we went
from who we were
to who we became
after "I do."

I realised we were
at the beginning,
when we said,
till death do us part,
in sickness and in health.

...promises.

I smile at you
in that photo,

on a London bench,
outside a redbrick
library.

Each day
I return to you:
your safety,
an opening,
an entrance.

Even through
the ups and downs.

Even after
distant migrations,
I can still remember
what it is
to come home.

Where I will burn

Bennachie

We drank tea from a flask
atop Bennachie, remember?

You showed me the land,
said, "this made me."

You pointed to the river,
understood it to be yours.

Every mile of every hill,
every crag woven into your DNA.

Had a memory of every coordinate,
and I longed for just some of it.

I longed to know a land like that,
close enough to feel at home

and for that home to love me back
like I was her one and only son.

Mother tongue

Mother of exiles, who calls us with beacon hand.
Goddess of ancient land, who understands
bloodshed and war.

Give us the feeling of May on the cusp of June
and all that we will yield in autumn's harvest.

Give us your all, in full no half measures,
as the pollen rises into spring clouds of possibility.

Show us how you understand that without us,
you would be broken and completely lost at sea.

Bestow on us a mother tongue, like the flames of Babel,
so we hear belonging as a universal language.

Let us understand you just enough, so as the bomb drops,
we will be able to move forward with our
God-forsaken lives.

Give us the secret compass that offers full belonging,
so, as we cut through gorse and thistle,
we can know the land.

Give us a moment of peace alone in the red-stained fields,
when we are amongst the scared and huddled masses.

Give us the promise of tomorrow and dreaming,
but more importantly, give us the words to write forever.

Ceremony

Or a poem for my writers group

The tea is steeping in cracked porcelain;
hibiscus, chamomile, Darjeeling and black
leaves brewing.

Their colourful oils like a spectrum,
creeping out the muslin and filling the pot with
mixed flavour.

If you took our community, steeped us all in one
copper container,
what would the drink taste like?

Many nations, shades, colours (all mapping out
diasporas)
melding into one watered-down history.

Left together to brew in collective trauma;
but we are not of one single origin, nor a single blend.

And, yet our tea is steeping in an ancient cauldron,
with leaves kept intact by the strength of our design.

Ramesh's magic carpet ride

Ramesh has a magic carpet
It takes him to new worlds
Where he is met with strange stares
Where his existence is weighed up
Like sumac, maize and cassava flour
Equally divvied up by all the possibilities
Of where he could "really" be from

Ramesh has a magic carpet
That gets him into trouble
When it trips up
Drunk men with two left feet
Whose white skin
Has gone bright pink from anger
Like foul chicken skin freshly plucked

Ramesh has a magic carpet
That he takes for rides
Above borders and over seas
He can see from on high
How the land does not have
Hard lines like the maps of textbooks
How the land has no borders at all

Ramesh has a magic carpet
That lets him take on the look
Of any brown man from anywhere
That lets angry drunk men
See him as any brown man

From anywhere
From wherever comes to mind

Ramesh can be any brown man
Can be Ramesh
Can be Andrés
Can be Salvador
Can be Panfilo
Can be any brown man

Ramesh has a magic carpet
That really is not magical
Because when he needs it
Desperate for its magic
In order to disappear
It does nothing to save him
Only causes him trouble

Ramesh does not have a magic carpet
Ramesh does not have a home
Ramesh does not belong
Ramesh can never belong
Because Ramesh is not Ramesh
Ramesh is every brown man

Endless

after Frantz Fanon

In the World through which I travel,
I am endlessly in search of myself
with no fixed point in mind.

No longer am I Luna, or Escobedo,
no longer a Muñoz, have since lost
Maldonado in my story.

When I landed in Basque country,
I could not even anchor Ordorica
to the bloodshed of my past.

I could not see myself in the vista
as desperate as I was.

I waded through marshland,
split weathered skin on sandstone,
dove into the harsh Atlantic cold.

None of these lands could reflect me,
each one turned their cheek,
whispering to go further, so I did.

In the World through which I travel,
I am continuously rewriting myself
with no fixed point in mind.

Belonging

In the spirit world there exists
a river like the Rio Grande
but is the Styx carrying its dead.

I press my face into its cold dark black
screaming out all the names that made me,
praying they'll claim me as their own.

Stout

I look at the pint – its clear delineation
of white and black.

I look at the flower boxes – a spring shower
of ivy, blue and pink mums, and bougainvillea.

I look into his eyes, grey with green veins,
granite cut artefacts from his hometown.

"Are you alright, you're awfully quiet?"

The world around is burning at a rapid pace,
and I have grown accustomed to merely scrolling past.

Death is everywhere cutting off our breath,
livestreaming our last minutes.

I take a giant sip, as a group of men hoot and holler
when the opposing team misses a penalty.

I look at another table, people taking posed selfies,
and I not far removed from this complacency.

Everyone scrolling, consuming, uploading
as a mad fiery anger begins to brew inside.

The sea is rising

There will be times you forget
how to swim, as your siblings
fall into troubled waters.

When the sea rises
and the tide rolls in
onto a bay of anxiety and chaos.

Standing at the harbour's edge
you'll try to recall instructions
for overcoming cold water shock.

You'll scream for them
to keep calm or keep swimming or
keep breathing or keep calm or
just please don't die.

As the water grows darker
as the waves grow choppier
and your mind is muddled
by constant overthinking...

You'll search for a lifesaver
to no avail, until you
finally remember:

I am the lifesaver.

There will be times you watch
your kin flailing in the sea
and need to throw yourself in.

There will be times the water tricks you
into thinking you can't swim
but remember you can.

I am the lifesaver.

You won't be able to do it all,
this isn't the point of life,
but you must make a start.

Your siblings are drowning
in a sea of tumult,
the water is rising fast.

I am the lifesaver.

Remember, it's not red nor white,
nor is it a ring-shaped circle,
the lifesaver is you,
it's time you jumped in.

The one who outcounts

Geese fly above me.
V-shaped; gravity pulling them into formation.

Geese fly south into the coldest depths of
winter light guides them across
the globe they see the world in ways
humans cannot gaggle together... don't.

But what of the goose straggling behind?
The one who outcounts the V-shaped form.
The one who never calls loudly but has so much to say.
The who took too long to fly the nest.

What of the straggler?

Who doesn't want to fly south to fly north
to fly south to fly over your mountains over your waves,
across your burning planes back and forth each season
forced to follow and never allowed to question nature.

What of his desires?

To fly east, to fly west, to rest, to burn the compass and
instead
fly crop circles into a slipstream that jettisons him toward
a nothingness, a void where he makes up for lost time
a void where he can get lost – give in to his desires.

Geese fly above me.

As muscle memory escapes my wings, as I forget how to fly
even as winter rolls in deep, as coldness fills my gullet,
and I drown in my own gaggle.

No more. Please.

Today, I will fly east toward the rising sun, toward its fiery
oranges
to let red wash over me in its angry embers,
until the pain becomes beautiful,
as I fly toward the place where I will burn the world down.

Epilogue

Mis raíces

We are in the desert, lips cracked,
mouth dried like freshly milled maize.

The ground sighs as if inconvenienced
by each of our steps over its thirsty ochre.

There are tall green nopales lined in neat rows,
reminding me how even here abundance is possible.

Grandfather asks me my thoughts of the land,
so, I ask him if this is where we come from:

Sí mijo, half of you is from this desert.

I lick my lips, parched like the earth,
take my boots off then my dirty socks.

Stomp my feet to the beat of the Jarabe Tapatío,
digging deeper into the soil with each kick.

"What are you doing?" asks my grandfather.

I want to be a nopal, Papá. I want to grow.

So, he leaves me, then returns with a shovel,
carefully plants me into this weathered landscape.

Afterward, he kisses me goodbye with such strength,
before patting my soft head, and in his touch, I know:

I will be fine here. All will be fine.

The desert is mine if I want it, here I'll learn how to grow.

And so, my grandfather begins the return journey alone,
the ground calls after him, but I stay quiet because I
know:

I will be fine here. All will be fine.

I am the true vine, and the desert is my gardener,
it's mine to inherit because I am of both land and root.

Notes

I'd like to extend my deepest gratitude to the following publications and platforms who gave early drafts of these poems a chance, and to the readers and listeners for supporting them:

Fringe of Colour Films – Mother in the community pool (film poem); *404 Ink Magazine* – Bottled Blue; *Lies, Dreaming* – These pyramids are houses for the dead (audio poem); *Broken Sleep Books* – Losing Myself; *Confluence Medway* – Hove; *Tapsalteerie* – Ceremony

'Amor,' 'Neroli Kiss,' and 'Bennachie' were written as part of a film poem funded through The Second Life grants scheme to celebrate the Edwin Morgan Centenary. Supported by Creative Scotland, The Saltire Society and The Edwin Morgan Trust (2021).

'We are young and still have time' was commissioned by Summerhall as part of '10 Years of Summerhall' (2021).

The poem *blessings* is inspired by George Mackay Brown's 'The Finished House' (*The Collected Poems of George Mackay Brown*, John Murray, 2005).

The poem *fresas* is inspired by Edwin Morgan's 'Strawberries' (*The Second Life*, Edinburgh University Press, 1968).

The repeat in the poem *Mother tongue* is inspired by Emma Lazarus' 'The New Colossus' written in 1883 to fundraise for the construction of the pedestal for the Statue of Liberty on New York City's Liberty Island.

The opening and closing stanzas in the poem *Endless* are inspired by Frantz Fanon's quote "In the World through which I travel, I am endlessly creating myself" (*Black Skin, White Masks,* Grove Press, 1967).

The last couplet in *Mis Raíces* is inspired by the biblical verse, "I am the true vine, and my Father is the gardener" (*New International Version*, John 15:1).

Acknowledgements

This collection was born out of love and loss – felt in tandem. I am grateful to have had these poems to buoy me through a particular difficult chapter of my life.

To the following people who helped me get to the source of that pain and unfurl its beauty, I offer these words:

I would like to first thank Laura Jones and Heather McDaid for saying 'yes' to the original iteration of this collection and for understanding it was in its infancy, still needing to grow. What a blessing to put my first body of work out through 404 Ink. Thank you for all you do to support emerging voices.

To Rachel Plummer, whose deft editorial eye helped shape this collection into a body of work that honours my intent, my deepest gratitude. Your original poetic advice shared on a rainy afternoon during *Solidarity On The Shore* is what led me to asking you to join this journey. I knew if ever I published a poetry collection, I would need you as the editor, so thank you for accompanying me.

To all the writers in the Scottish BAME Writers Network, and our wondrous Writers of Colour group, thank you for inspiring me endlessly. You know who you are!

To Lighthouse Books for being a refuge for so many of us, thank you for your warmth and solidarity.

To Hannah Lavery and Nadine Aisha Jassat, I offer my love and respect. How lucky I am to count you both as dear friends, mentors, and guiding lights as I navigate this exciting but strange world of verse and performance.

Other wonderful writers I must say thank you to include Alycia Pirmohamed, Jeda Pearl Lewis, Dean Atta, Jenni Fagan, Damian Barr, Jess Brough, and Etzali Hernández. Writing is a solo act but all of you have made it a little less lonely.

To my dearest friends Emma, Harriet, Cyndi, Jasmine, Merran, Fern, Kaeli, and Meagan, thank you for your constant support and cheering me along the way. Our bonds are fiercely strong, extending over many years and many borders!

To my parents, Salvador and Sonia, thank you for giving me the space to create, for supporting my love of books, for guarding me in fervent prayer and for believing that I could achieve my dreams. I love you both so much.

To my grandparents, los quiero mucho. Gracias por su apoyo y todo su amor – to be an immigrant is a brave and defiant act of hope and my four grandparents have always proven that through how they live(d).

To my siblings, Salvador, Selyssa, and Enrique, thank you for letting me be my weird, aloof self and for understanding my need to find myself outside the worlds we were born into. I hope you know where you live in these poems.

To my husband Kevin, we often speak without words and that is the greatest language that I share with anyone. Thank you for being a place I can always return to – I am sure you know which poems are yours.

To my Scottish family (The Guyans and The Marnochs) for being a haim in a place that doesn't always feel like haim and for sharing Bennachie with me – I thank you!

To those of us, who are immigrants, or part of diasporas, children/grandchildren of immigrants (including my very big Ordorica/Maldonado/Luna/Escobedo familia), these poems are yours.

To my queer family, my found family, these poems are yours.

To you, the reader, thank you for going on this journey.

Con todo mi amor,

Andrés

About the Author

Daniel McGowan

Andrés N. Ordorica is a queer Latinx poet and writer based in Edinburgh, who creates worlds filled with characters who are from neither here nor there (ni de aquí, ni de allá). Publishing credits include *The Skinny*, *Bella Caledonia*, *Confluence Medway*, *Somewhere: For Us*, and *Gutter*. In 2020, he was awarded a Second Life grant through the Edwin Morgan Trust. His novel in progress *The Places We Will Go* was longlisted for the 2021 Mo Siewcharran Prize.